VALENTINE'S BOOMER

Red Hot & Slightly Irregular

by

A L Manley

Ink-Twenty

Valentine's Boom
Red Hot & Slightly Irregular

ISBN: 9798993554495

Published by **Ink-Twenty**
Richmond, Virginia
Ink-Twenty.Studio

🖤 CHAPTER I

What Created Valentine's Day (And Why We're Still Dealing With It)

Let's be honest right out of the gate.

Valentine's Day did not begin as a holiday.

It began as an idea that simply refused to stay in its lane.

Yes, yes — there was a Saint Valentine somewhere back there in the historical fog, and yes, poets eventually showed up, which is always when things start getting complicated. But the Valentine's Day you and I know — the one with rules, pressure, color coordination, and emotional accounting — is not ancient. It is modern. Extremely modern. And like many modern inventions, it was perfected in America by people who understood packaging, timing, and just how uncomfortable silence can be.

Enter Hallmark.

Hallmark did not invent love. They did not invent romance. They didn't even invent longing. What they did invent — and this is not nothing — was the idea that love should be expressed on schedule, inside a folded card, preferably with embossing, possibly foil, and ideally something you could not have written yourself without breaking into a cold sweat.

Before greeting cards became standard, people either spoke from the heart or didn't speak at all. Which, frankly, solved a great many problems. Hallmark arrived and said, What if we helped? And by help, they meant professionalization.

Emotion, but tidy.
Sentiment, but pre-approved.
Feelings, but with spellcheck.

By the middle of the twentieth century, greeting cards were no longer optional. They were expected. Valentine's Day stopped being about what you felt and became about whether you showed up correctly. And Boomers — all of us — were born directly into that system. No warning label. No opt-out clause.

Hallmark's rise aligned almost perfectly with the Baby Boom, and no, that was not coincidence. Millions of children. Millions of households. Millions of moments suddenly needing marking, managing, and monetizing. Valentine's Day was perfect for this. It was compact. Predictable. Teachable. You could introduce it early and reinforce it annually.

Which is exactly what happened.

Boomers didn't learn Valentine's Day from lovers.
We learned it from teachers.

Classrooms were our first training ground. Everyone gets a card, even if you don't like them. Especially if you don't like them. Hearts mean love. Red means serious. Pink means safe. Glitter means someone's parent got involved. Names must be written carefully. Envelopes must be counted. Observations must be made quietly but thoroughly.

That wasn't romance.

That was conditioning.

Hallmark understood something fundamental long before the rest of us caught on: emotion is easier when someone gives you the words. They didn't just sell cards — they sold scripts. They taught us what affection should sound like, how long it should be, and when it should arrive. They made feelings acceptable as long as they fit neatly inside a message someone else had already approved.

And Boomers bought in.

Completely.

By the time we were old enough to date, Valentine's Day already came with an internal checklist we never consciously agreed to but somehow all memorized. Card. Candy. Flowers if things were "serious." Jewelry if things were very serious. Each escalation carried meaning, whether anyone said it out loud or not. You weren't just giving something — you were communicating. Sometimes several things at once. Occasionally things you absolutely did not mean.

A card could say I like you.
Flowers could say I'm trying.
Jewelry could say We should talk.

Valentine's Day became less about love and more about interpretation.

Hallmark thrived because Boomers thrived. We grew up, paired off, had children, and then repeated the cycle without even noticing we were doing it. We bought Valentine's cards for classmates, spouses, children, parents, teachers, coworkers, and eventually ourselves. The holiday became generational muscle memory. You didn't question it. You just knew February 14th was coming and that you were expected to acknowledge it somehow.

Did Hallmark succeed because of Boomers?

In large part, yes.

We were the first generation raised entirely inside the greeting-card economy. We normalized it. We institutionalized it. We turned it into tradition. We taught our children the same rituals we had learned — sometimes sincerely, sometimes with a raised eyebrow, often while insisting we "weren't really into Valentine's Day" as we placed the cards carefully into the cart.

And here's the thing that matters.

None of this makes us foolish.

It makes us fluent.

We understand Valentine's Day because we watched it being assembled in real time. We lived through its peak years, its excesses, its performative phases, and its quieter evolutions. We learned when it was sweet, when it was stressful, and when it stopped meaning what it once did.

Valentine's Day didn't create our romantic lives — but it absolutely shaped how we expressed them. It taught us to equate love with effort, visibility, and timing. It taught us that affection should be acknowledged publicly, even when it was deeply private. It taught us that not participating was, in itself, a statement.

And now — decades later — we get to pause.

We get to look at the whole thing with perspective. With humor. With lived experience. We get to decide what we want to keep and what we're finally ready to let go.

Because this book is not about rejecting Valentine's Day. It's about understanding it.

About recognizing how it shaped us, amused us, embarrassed us, occasionally disappointed us, and sometimes surprised us. About tracing the line from construction-paper hearts to grown-up expectations — and asking, quietly, Do I still want to do this the same way?

Once you know where something came from, you're free to decide what it's for.

And that — questioning the structure without losing the sentiment — is a very Boomer move.

Headphones on.
Door closed.
Let's keep talking.

❤️ CHAPTER II

Fads, Gimmicks, and the Many Ways We Tried to Look Normal

If Valentine's Day was the lesson, the fads were the homework.

And Boomers did a lot of homework.

Not because we were eager students — but because there were consequences. Social ones. Emotional ones. Public ones. Valentine's Day wasn't something you casually participated in. It was something you navigated. Carefully. With awareness. With a vague sense that someone was always watching, even when no one technically was.

Boomers didn't just grow up with Valentine's Day.
We grew up trying to survive it.

Every decade handed us a new set of instructions, most of them unspoken. New materials. New rules. New ways to prove we were doing this correctly. And every one of those ways came with the same underlying risk: doing it wrong.

Which, of course, we often did.
Publicly.

The fifties laid the foundation, and they did it politely. This was the era of wholesomeness with sharp elbows. Valentine's Day meant lace-edged cards, pastel palettes, and language that sounded like it had passed through several committees before being approved. Boys were "fellows." Girls were "darlings." Everyone was smiling. No one perspired. No one acknowledged desire directly.

And yet — somehow — everyone understood exactly what everything meant.

Candy hearts arrived early and never left. Those tiny chalky tablets with messages like Be Mine and Call Me were less candy than communication devices. Emotional shorthand. You didn't eat them because they tasted good. You ate them because they proved someone had handed you something. Boomers learned early that romance was not about flavor.

It was about evidence.

By the time we reached elementary school, Valentine's Day had become an organized operation. Desks were cleared. Construction paper appeared as if summoned. Paste made a dramatic return. Shoe boxes were transformed into mailboxes, decorated with hearts, cupids, and unchecked optimism.

Everyone was supposed to give everyone a card.

Which sounded fair until you noticed that some cards were clearly chosen with intention, while others were distributed with efficiency. You could tell who had been thought about and who had been handled quickly near the end of the box.

The cards themselves were tiny masterpieces of social coding. Superheroes meant safe. Animals meant neutral. Cartoons meant friendly. Anything with glitter meant someone's parent had thoughts. And if a card had your name written extra neatly — not just signed, but written — you noticed.

You always noticed.

Then came the sixties, and things loosened up just enough to make everyone uneasy.

Suddenly Valentine's Day wasn't just cute — it was cool-adjacent. Colors got bolder. Fonts got louder. Humor crept in. Cards started making jokes, which meant feelings were now allowed as long as they arrived disguised as sarcasm. This was a revelation for Boomers. We learned that if you couldn't say something directly, you could always say it sideways.

Which, as it turns out, is a skill we have never entirely given up.

School dances appeared. Not actual dances — supervised dances. Valentine's-themed events held in gyms decorated with crepe paper and optimism. Lighting that did no one any favors. Music slow enough to make standing still feel like a personal failure.

Couples swayed awkwardly. Singles perfected the art of pretending not to care. Everyone watched everyone else while pretending not to.

And then there were carnations.

Carnations were the flower of choice because they were affordable, durable, and just serious enough to suggest intention without committing to anything irreversible. A red carnation said one thing. A pink one said another. A white one said absolutely nothing helpful at all.

Receiving one during the school day meant walking the halls holding your social status in plant form.

By the seventies, Boomers were teenagers, and Valentine's Day officially became complicated.

This was the era of notes folded into impossible shapes, passed between classes like classified documents. "Do you like me?" was no longer acceptable. It had to be encoded. Check yes. Check no. Check maybe. Maybe meant panic.

Conversation hearts gave way to mixtapes — and mixtapes were not casual. You didn't just hand someone music. You curated your emotions in the precise order you wanted them understood. Song choice mattered. Sequence mattered. Side A versus Side B mattered.

If the tape ran long, that meant something.
If it ended abruptly, that meant something else.

Advertisements leaned hard into romance during these years. Everything was suddenly Valentine's branded. Perfume ads implied that love could be sprayed on. Jewelry ads suggested deadlines. Candy ads promised that sugar could fix conversations you hadn't had.

School Valentine's traditions escalated accordingly. Singing telegrams. Balloon deliveries. Roses handed out during homeroom. Nothing says emotional vulnerability like watching someone else receive something while you suddenly become very invested in reading.

First loves lived here.
So did first heartbreaks.

Valentine's Day had a unique talent for amplifying whatever you were already feeling. If things were good, the day felt cinematic. If things were uncertain, it felt like a test you hadn't studied for. And if things were over, Valentine's Day arrived anyway — cheerful, relentless, and deeply unhelpful.

Boomers learned timing from all of this.
We learned anticipation.
We learned dread.
We learned that romance often comes with witnesses — and that witnesses have opinions.

Through it all, the gimmicks kept coming. Stuffed animals holding hearts. Cards that played music. Cards that popped open. Cards that talked back. Cards that said far too much for their size.

Valentine's Day grew louder. Brighter. Harder to ignore.

And yet — somehow — we loved it.

Not because it was perfect.
Because it was shared.

Everyone was in it together. Everyone knew the rules, even when we pretended not to. Valentine's Day became a shared cultural embarrassment, and there is comfort in that. There's something bonding about collectively navigating a situation no one fully understands but everyone is expected to perform.

🖤 CHAPTER III

Boomers at School (Ages 10–17): Where Valentine's Day Got Teeth

This is the chapter where Valentine's Day stopped being adorable and started keeping score.

Up until then, it had at least pretended to be sweet. Manageable. Something you could survive with construction paper and a little glue. But somewhere between elementary school and adolescence, the holiday sharpened its edges and began quietly evaluating us.

Elementary school Valentine's were designed to look fair. Everyone gives everyone a card. That was the rule. It was announced. It was enforced. It was laminated and sent home in backpacks.

The problem, of course, was that children are terrible at equality.

Even at ten, we could tell which cards had been selected carefully and which ones were grabbed at the last minute from the bottom of the box. We knew which ones came from a multipack and which ones had been purchased individually, with intent. We didn't need instruction. We were already fluent.

The shoe-box mailbox was our first lesson in personal branding. Some kids went minimalist. Clean lines. Function over form. Others went full interior decorator. Pipe cleaners. Lace paper. Glitter applied with enthusiasm and absolutely no concern for long-term consequences.

Your box said things about you.
And sometimes about your home life.

Distribution day arrived with the energy of polite chaos. Teachers hovered, attempting neutrality. Children hovered harder. Everyone pretended not to count. Everyone counted. We watched the flow of cards with the intensity of seasoned analysts. Who got more. Who got fewer. Who got the ones with care. Who got the ones with speed.

You learned quickly that "Happy Valentine's Day" was neutral. "From" plus your name was friendly. Writing someone's name instead of just signing yours was intentional. Writing it in cursive meant you were either brave or reckless. Hearts were high risk. Stickers were flirtation. And if someone added extra hearts, you told no one and thought about it constantly.

Constantly.

Then came junior high.

Which was less a developmental stage and more a social experiment that should have been shut down early.

This is where Valentine's Day went underground. Everything became covert. Notes were passed like contraband. Folded into triangles. Or squares. Or shapes that required advanced geometry and emotional nerve. Messages were deliberately vague. "Do you like me?" was far too exposed. It became "Who do you like?" which was always a trap.

Crushes multiplied. Confidence evaporated. Everyone wanted proof, but no one wanted to ask directly. So we built systems. Entire communication infrastructures designed to avoid saying what we meant. Signals. Intermediaries. Strategic silence.

It was excellent preparation for adulthood.

Junior high Valentine's Day was ninety percent anxiety and ten percent gum. If a note made it to you intact, that alone was a victory. If it didn't, the humiliation was immediate and thorough. Lessons were learned quickly and rarely forgotten.

And just when you thought it couldn't get more complicated, high school arrived and brought an audience.

Now Valentine's Day was public. Highly visible. Carnations appeared during class like floral subpoenas. Balloons floated through hallways announcing feelings that had not been fully processed. Deliveries happened in real time, in front of peers who had opinions and memories and absolutely nothing else to do.

If you received something, everyone noticed.
If you didn't, you noticed louder.

This is where Boomers learned that romance is often performed for bystanders.

Couples suddenly had to do Valentine's correctly. Not just feel it — perform it. Singles perfected the art of pretending they were above it while desperately hoping someone would slip up and reveal the whole system as flawed. The cafeteria on February 14th was a master class in denial, posture, and overconfidence.

And then there were the dances.

Valentine's dances were held in gyms, which should tell you everything you need to know. Streamers taped to basketball hoops. Crepe paper attempting romance. Music slow enough to induce panic. Lighting that made everyone look like they were reconsidering their life choices.

People leaned against walls waiting for something to happen. Which meant nothing happened until someone with courage, curiosity, or questionable judgment broke the stalemate.

When dancing occurred, it was awkward. Earnest. Unforgettable for all the wrong reasons. Hands hovered. Feet shuffled. Someone always misread the moment. Someone always stepped on someone else.

And yet — for a few minutes — you were inside the myth. The one you'd been sold since childhood. The idea that

Valentine's Day might deliver something transformative if you just stood still long enough.

First loves appeared around here. Sometimes quietly. Sometimes dramatically. Valentine's Day didn't invent them, but it absolutely exaggerated them. If things were good, the day felt cinematic. If things were uncertain, it felt like a pop quiz you hadn't studied for. And if things had just ended, Valentine's Day arrived anyway, cheerful and unbothered, as if personally mocking you.

Boomers learned endurance here.

We learned how to get through the day when things didn't go our way. We learned how to accept disappointment with humor because the alternative was melodrama, and none of us had the energy for that. We learned that rejection rarely comes with instructions or context.

We also learned comedy.

Because laughter was the only reasonable response to a holiday that asked twelve- and thirteen-year-olds to navigate emotional nuance using candy and construction paper. Humor became armor. Self-awareness became survival.

By the time we graduated, Valentine's Day had already done its work. It had trained us to manage expectations. To read rooms. To protect ourselves just enough while still leaving space for hope.

It taught us that wanting something doesn't guarantee anything.

And that sometimes the most romantic thing you can do is make it through the day with your dignity mostly intact.

What followed would only get more complicated.

And somehow, we were ready.

🖤 CHAPTER IV

Boomers as Young Adults (18–29): Romance, Rent, and Waking Up Employed

This is the chapter where Valentine's Day ran straight into adulthood and chipped a tooth.

One day you were in school.
The next day you woke up and went to work.

That was it.

No soft landing. No orientation video. No kindly voice saying, You might want to ease into this. You opened your eyes, put on clothes that suddenly meant something different, and joined traffic with a purpose you hadn't fully negotiated. You were now employed. Which meant you were also tired. Permanently. But proud.

If you were in college, Valentine's Day landed right in the middle of everything else you were barely managing. Papers due. Exams looming. Laundry unresolved. Romance lived between classes and part-time jobs, fueled by caffeine and optimism. You loved passionately, but inexpensively. Valentine's meant pizza, candles you already owned, and the sincere belief that someday you would laugh about this from a nicer couch.

You didn't need much.
You had time.
Or at least you thought you did.

Knock, knock.
Who's there?
Tuition.

Tuition who?
Tuition me that love is free, because everything else is not.

Then graduation happened, which felt ceremonial right up until the next morning.

That's when it hit you.

No one was asking what time your first class was. They were asking where you were. And why you weren't there yet. You learned quickly that mornings were no longer theoretical. They were contractual.

Valentine's Day now had to fit around a full-time job. Around commutes. Around bosses who did not care about romance unless it interfered with productivity. Evenings were suddenly shorter than advertised. Weekends disappeared faster than expected. You learned the strange arithmetic of adulthood, where eight hours of work somehow required ten hours of recovery.

Boomers entered the workforce when jobs still promised things. Stability. Loyalty. Pensions people discussed seriously, as if they were guaranteed. You dressed for work. You packed lunches. You learned how to look busy even when you weren't entirely sure what you were doing.

And you were doing a lot of things.

Valentine's Day squeezed itself into this new life with mixed results. It competed with deadlines and exhaustion and the quiet realization that staying in was sometimes the most romantic option available.

Knock, knock.
Who's there?
Budget.
Budget who?

Budget doesn't include flowers, but I remembered your name.

Dating culture in young adulthood came with rules no one explained but everyone enforced. You were supposed to care, but not appear desperate. Plan something thoughtful, but not expensive. Be spontaneous, but make reservations. Valentine's Day became a test, and no one provided the study guide.

Romance competed with roommates, shared kitchens, and furniture that technically belonged to someone else. Valentine's gifts became creative out of necessity. Candles pulled double duty. Cooking dinner at home was framed as intimate, which was fortunate because restaurants were booked and you were tired.

Knock, knock.
Who's there?
Commitment.
Commitment who?
Commitment sounds great, but let's not rush Valentine's.

Work changed everything.

Valentine's Day followed you into the office, where it became quietly awkward. Cards circulated that said nothing specific to anyone. Candy bowls appeared with invisible rules. Flowers showed up on desks and immediately became a topic of conversation that had nothing to do with flowers.

Romance learned to behave under fluorescent lighting.

You learned which coworkers overshared and which ones noticed everything. You learned that office Valentine's etiquette was a minefield best crossed quickly and with neutral expressions.

Knock, knock.
Who's there?
Overtime.
Overtime who?
Overtime means dinner is cancelled but I still like you.

Dating after work required stamina. You met tired. You talked tired. You tried to be charming when your brain had already gone home. Valentine's Day shifted from grand gestures to measurable effort. Showing up counted. Staying awake counted more.

Advertisements during this era did not help. They suggested that love could be purchased, upgraded, and delivered on time. Jewelry ads implied deadlines. Card ads implied guilt. Everyone else looked like they were doing Valentine's Day better than you, which was impressive considering everyone else was also winging it.

Knock, knock.
Who's there?
Adulting.
Adulting who?
Adulting is hard, let's just split dessert.

By the late seventies and early eighties, Boomers were juggling careers, relationships, and the growing suspicion that no one actually knew what they were doing. Valentine's Day adjusted. It became negotiated. Dinner or movie. Card or no card. Big gesture or mutual agreement to lower expectations.

Romance became more conversational. Less ceremonial. You talked about things. Money. Schedules. Energy. You learned that love didn't pause for uncertainty. People moved for jobs. People worked late. People missed things. Valentine's Day sometimes arrived when one of you was stressed, distracted, or questioning everything.

Love had to be flexible or it didn't survive.

If you were single, Valentine's Day felt louder. Coworkers asked questions. Commercials followed you. You learned how to shrug convincingly and buy yourself something without turning it into a statement.

Knock, knock.
Who's there?
Single.
Single who?
Single tonight, but I brought snacks.

Some Valentine's Days were wonderful. Some were forgettable. Some were quietly devastating. But all of them unfolded against the backdrop of paychecks, schedules, and the slow understanding that love now had to coexist with real life.

Knock, knock.
Who's there?
Stress.

Stress who?

Stress is why this Valentine's card is late but heartfelt.

Knock, knock.

Who's there?

Career.

Career who?

Career is important, but can we still split dessert?

And finally, the joke that followed us everywhere:

Knock, knock.

Who's there?

Reality.

Reality who?

Reality says romance is great, but the alarm is set for six.

These years mattered.

They taught Boomers how to balance affection with obligation. Humor with fatigue. Hope with realism. Valentine's Day didn't disappear during young adulthood — it matured. It learned how to live alongside work, responsibility, and the quiet pride of being able to support yourself.

Young adulthood didn't kill romance.

It just made it earn its keep.

And somehow, we did too.

🖤 CHAPTER V

Boomers With Children: Romance Goes Quiet

This is the chapter where Valentine's Day stopped asking for attention and started waiting its turn.

Not because love disappeared.
Because it got crowded.

Once children entered the picture, romance didn't leave the room — it just moved to the background. Still playing. Still there. Just quieter. Occasionally drowned out by cartoons, carpools, and the mysterious stickiness that seemed to migrate from surface to surface with no clear plan.

Valentine's Day began arriving with a different energy. Less anticipation. More calculation. You still noticed it was coming — the calendar didn't stop working — but instead of wondering what will happen, you wondered something far more practical:

How much effort is reasonable under the circumstances?

Children changed the calendar. Not officially — February still came right after January — but emotionally. Valentine's Day became something you worked around instead of toward. You were busy helping someone else cut hearts out of construction paper while quietly wondering if anyone remembered that you, too, were a person with a pulse.

Romance had competition now.
Serious competition.

Children required logistics. Timing. Snacks. Supervision. Valentine's plans had to survive nap schedules, homework deadlines, forgotten permission slips, and a level of exhaustion that could not be reasoned with. Love was still present, but it had to be efficient.

This is when Valentine's Day gestures got smaller.

A card left on the counter.
Chocolate purchased during a regular grocery run.
Dinner at home because leaving the house felt ambitious.

And that was okay.

Mostly.

Love during this phase expressed itself through function. You showed affection by showing up. By handling things. By knowing where everything was — including the things no one else could ever find. You didn't need grand gestures. You needed help.

Sometimes Valentine's Day passed quietly, acknowledged with a look that said, Yes, we see it. No, not this year. Sometimes it didn't get acknowledged at all.

Which, as it turns out, is also information.

Children also reintroduced Valentine's Day into the house — aggressively.

Suddenly there were school projects again. Bags of candy. Classroom rules about how many cards were required and which snacks were allowed. Valentine's Day became something you facilitated rather than participated in. You moved from center stage to support staff.

You bought the supplies.
You signed the permission slips.

You stayed up late assembling something that would be briefly appreciated.

And later, you ate the leftover candy at the kitchen counter, standing, wondering how that became your role.

As children grew older, Valentine's Day shifted again.

When kids became teenagers, romance returned to the household — just not yours. Valentine's Day now involved rides, curfews, and concern. You watched history repeat itself from a careful distance, recognizing the expressions, the nerves, the hope.

This part was unsettling.

You remembered too much.

You wanted to say something helpful. Something wise. Something that might spare them unnecessary heartbreak. But nothing sounded right. Valentine's Day had already taught you that advice is rarely welcome in matters of the heart.

So you stayed quiet.
You made snacks.
You waited up.

Your own Valentine's Day during these years was often postponed, rescheduled, or quietly minimized. You were tired. Not metaphorically. Actually tired. Romance now had to negotiate with energy levels, schedules, and the simple reality that silence could be preferable to small talk.

Sometimes it worked.
Sometimes it didn't.
Sometimes it took a rain check that was never cashed.

This wasn't failure.

It was reality.

Love during the child-rearing years was durable rather than dramatic. It didn't announce itself. It carried groceries. It remembered appointments. It kept going even when no one said thank you. It lived in the unglamorous middle — the place where life actually happens.

Valentine's Day during this phase didn't need to be loud.

It needed to be patient.

And patience, it turns out, is a form of romance that doesn't photograph well but lasts.

This is also where Boomers began to recalibrate expectations. Valentine's Day stopped being a measure of devotion and became more of a check-in. A moment to notice where you were. Together or apart. Tired or steady. Connected or simply coexisting.

Sometimes you missed the old versions. The anticipation. The novelty. The possibility.
And sometimes you were deeply relieved they were gone.

Because love with children in the house was no longer theoretical. It was proven daily, in ways no card could ever capture.

Valentine's Day didn't disappear during these years.

It just learned how to whisper.

And you learned how to listen differently.

🖤 CHAPTER VI

Boomers With Teenagers: Watching the Movie From the Lobby

This is the chapter where Valentine's Day comes back into the house wearing different clothes and speaking a language you do not fully understand.

By the time Boomers were raising teenagers, the holiday had changed. Not completely — hearts were still involved, anticipation was still involved — but the experience was no longer analog. It was mediated. Filtered. Observed through screens. Conducted at a speed that made reflection optional and restraint feel almost quaint.

And you noticed.

Boomer parents watched their teenagers navigate Valentine's Day with a mixture of recognition and disbelief. The emotions were familiar. Almost painfully so. The methods were not. It felt like watching a remake of a movie you remembered vividly, except the dialogue was faster, the soundtrack was louder, and the pacing made you tired just thinking about it.

When we were teenagers, Valentine's Day happened in real time. You waited. You wondered. You stared at the phone like it might eventually blink first. You risked embarrassment face-to-face. If something went wrong, it went wrong publicly — but it was contained. The audience was limited to whoever happened to be nearby at the time.

Our teenagers did not have that luxury.

By the late eighties and nineties, Valentine's Day lived everywhere at once. Messages didn't get folded and passed — they arrived instantly. Feelings were communicated digitally, sometimes without tone, sometimes without thought, sometimes without mercy. Rejection didn't take hours

or days anymore. It took seconds. Sometimes it took a single word. Sometimes it took silence, which somehow said more.

Boomer parents recognized the feelings immediately. The hope.

The nerves.

The relentless overanalysis of every word.

What startled us wasn't the emotion.

It was the scale.

And the speed.

The mall became the neutral ground.

For Boomers, the mall had once been freedom. Climate-controlled independence. A place where you could wander without supervision, be seen without committing to anything, and maybe — just maybe — run into someone on purpose while pretending it was an accident. The mall was possibility with a food court.

For our teenagers, the mall was still a gathering place, but it carried more weight. Valentine's week at the mall was practically a field study in adolescent behavior.

You saw it all.

Groups of teens pretending not to care.
Couples walking just close enough to signal status.
Gift bags from chain stores that meant something very

specific.

Food courts full of emotion disguised as french fries.

The mall was where Valentine's gifts got evaluated in public. Where balloons floated like announcements. Where candy became a statement. Where who bought what, from where, and for whom mattered far more than anyone admitted.

Boomers watching this had flashbacks.

We remembered the pressure. The comparisons. The way a holiday could suddenly feel like a referendum on your worth. The difference was that our version ended when we went home. Theirs followed them — into cars, onto phones, into bedrooms, into conversations that never fully shut off.

Technology didn't just change communication.

It removed the pauses.

There was no waiting by the phone anymore. No wondering if someone would call. Messages arrived instantly. Silence also arrived instantly. Everything felt urgent. Everything felt amplified. Valentine's Day now came with a running commentary — likes, replies, read receipts, screenshots.

Boomer parents stood on the sidelines trying to look calm.

You wanted to say things like, This won't matter someday.
You didn't say it.
You knew better.

Because it mattered now.

Teen Valentine's also changed how parents experienced the holiday. Suddenly February 14th wasn't about your relationship at all. It was about logistics. Rides. Curfews. Where they were going. Who they were with. When they'd be back. It was about worrying quietly and hoping your child would be kind — and be treated kindly in return.

You remembered your own teenage Valentine's with surprising clarity during these years. The ache of wanting something to happen. The sting when it didn't. The thrill when it did. Watching your children move through those same emotional landscapes reopened files you hadn't planned on accessing.

And yet, there was distance too.

Their world was louder. Faster. More exposed. They navigated feelings with an audience that never logged off. The mall, the phone, the screen — everything was connected. Valentine's Day didn't have edges anymore. It spilled.

Boomers learned restraint here.

You learned when to step in and when to step back. When to offer perspective and when to offer snacks instead. You learned that your job wasn't to fix Valentine's Day for your teenager. It was to survive it with them. To be present without hovering. To care without crowding.

And maybe — gently — to remind them that a holiday built on candy and marketing does not get the final word on their worth.

Valentine's Day with teenagers in the house was not nostalgic.

It was reflective.

You saw your past, their present, and a future you hoped would be kinder to them than it sometimes was to you. You realized that while the tools had changed, the feelings had not. Hearts still raced. Expectations still rose. Disappointments still landed.

Only now, you were watching from the other side.

From the lobby.

And for the first time, you understood just how much courage it takes to sit there quietly and let the movie play.

🩶 CHAPTER VI½

Licensed to Panic:

Boomers, Teen Driving, and the DMV That Learned the Hard Way

Before we move on, we need to talk about driving.

Not casually.
Not nostalgically.
Properly.

Because Valentine's Day with teenagers is one thing. Valentine's Day with teenagers who have driver's licenses is another category entirely. Possibly its own medical condition. Possibly something that should come with a waiver and a waiting room.

Boomers did not ease into driving.

We were handed keys.

That's not a metaphor. That's a memory.

When Boomers became teenagers, getting a driver's license wasn't just a milestone — it was liberation with paperwork. You didn't "earn" it in the modern sense. You didn't log hours or pass through layers of supervision. You demonstrated, briefly, that you could turn left without panic and stop at a sign without striking anything important or alive.

That was it.

You were released into the wild.

There were no graduated licenses. No provisional phases. No nighttime restrictions. No passenger limits. No laminated charts taped to refrigerators. You passed a test and suddenly you were responsible for a moving vehicle, other people's children, and your own deeply unexamined judgment.

The system trusted you.

This was... optimistic.

Boomer teens learned to drive in cars the size of studio apartments. Bench seats that slid whether you wanted them to or not. Suspensions with opinions. Brakes that required planning. No cup holders, because hydration had not yet entered the cultural conversation. Seat belts were optional. Helmets were theoretical. Safety was something you assumed would simply… happen.

And somehow, we survived.

Barely.

We drove everywhere. To school. To work. To the mall. To nowhere in particular. Driving wasn't just transportation — it was freedom, identity, therapy, and occasionally a substitute for conversation you weren't ready to have.

You drove because you could.
You drove because you needed to think.
You drove because sitting still felt like missing something.

Valentine's Day transportation depended entirely on who had access to a car and whose parents were the least likely to ask follow-up questions. Plans were made around keys, not calendars.

The car was the date.

Fast forward one generation.

Boomer parents watched their teenagers approach driving under a completely different set of rules — because the system had learned from us. Thoroughly. Intensely. Possibly with charts, color coding, and meetings that ran long.

By the time our kids reached driving age, the Department of Motor Vehicles had opinions. Strong ones. Carefully documented ones. There were graduated licenses. Provisional licenses. Nighttime restrictions. Passenger limits. Rules about rules.

The DMV no longer trusted teenagers.

Especially Boomer teenagers, in retrospect.

And honestly?

That's fair.

Boomer parents recognized immediately that this wasn't just bureaucracy. It was institutional memory. Somewhere, someone had looked at accident statistics from the seventies and said, Absolutely not doing that again.

Our teenagers had to log hours. Practice turns. Take classes. Watch videos that made driving look like a montage of regret, cautionary music, and poor decision-making. We did not watch those videos.

We were the reason those videos existed.

Which made watching our teens drive a uniquely layered experience.

Comforting, because they were trained.
Terrifying, because they were still teenagers.

Boomer parents became passengers for the first time in decades, and it showed. We braced. We inhaled sharply. We commented on braking. We pretended to be calm while discovering muscles we didn't know could clench.

We learned very quickly that saying, You're doing great, actually meant, I am gripping the door handle internally and reconsidering every life choice that led to this moment.

Driving with your teenager is an exercise in restraint. You see everything. You feel everything. You say almost nothing. Or too much. It's hard to tell in the moment.

Valentine's Day entered this situation as a logistical puzzle.

Who was driving whom.

What time they'd be back.

Whether the car had gas.

Whether the car would return at all.

Teen Valentine's plans now involved curfews, routes, contingency plans, and texts that said Leaving now and Almost there, which were meant to be reassuring but rarely were. We stared at phones the way we once stared at clocks, negotiating patience with anxiety.

Boomer parents remembered our own Valentine's driving vividly during this phase. The late-night drives. The long conversations that felt monumental at the time. The parked cars. The questionable decisions we defended with confidence.

We realized — with startling clarity — that our parents had been far calmer than we deserved.

The DMV, meanwhile, continued refining the process. More testing. More oversight. More restrictions. It was as if the entire system had quietly agreed that one generation of free-range teenage drivers was sufficient.

Boomers didn't need this explained.

We were the control group.

Driving, like Valentine's Day, became another place where Boomers saw the contrast between past and present clearly. We had grown up with trust. Our kids grew up with structure. We had freedom. They had safety protocols.

Neither approach was perfect.

But both shaped how we loved, dated, and showed up for one another.

Because driving was never just about transportation. It was about independence. About access. About possibility. About being able to say yes — or no — on your own terms. It was about choosing when to go and when to stay, without asking permission.

Valentine's Day, for teenagers, still depended on that freedom. It just arrived now with more rules, more planning, and significantly more parental awareness.

Boomer parents learned to let go here. Carefully. Incrementally. With GPS.

We watched our children drive off into their own versions of youth, carrying the same hope and nerves we once had

— just under better supervision, reflective tape, and a watchful eye that didn't sleep.

And maybe that was progress.

Or maybe it was simply what happens when a generation lives long enough to see the consequences of its own joyrides.

Either way, the DMV remembers.

And so do we.

🖤 CHAPTER VII

The Boomer Reset: So Long, Stay in Touch, Don't Move Back

This is the chapter nobody prepares you for.

Not really.
Not honestly.

People talk about it in passing, usually with a smile that doesn't quite commit. You'll love having the house to yourselves again. So much freedom. You'll finally get your life back.

All of that is true.

And also incomplete.

You spend years waiting for this moment. Complaining about it. Fantasizing about it. Counting down to it during especially loud dinners or especially quiet moments when you realize you haven't finished a thought in weeks. You imagine the freedom vividly.

And then it happens.

The house empties.
The car pulls away.
The door closes.

And suddenly the thing you wanted very badly arrives carrying feelings you did not order.

Empty nesting is a strange emotional cocktail.
Relief, served neat.

Sadness, served unexpectedly.
Freedom, with a twist.

You wanted them gone.
You did not want them gone.

When children leave — for college, for work, for life — the silence arrives first. Not dramatic silence. Not cinematic silence. Just absence. The refrigerator doesn't empty as fast. The laundry basket stops reproducing. The house feels larger without changing size.

It's disorienting.

Boomers adjust quickly.
And slowly.
Often at the same time.

At first, there's enthusiasm. Real enthusiasm. This is it. This is your time. You can finally do what you want, when you want, without coordinating calendars or explaining yourself. You can eat dinner at odd hours. You can watch something uninterrupted. You can leave the room without narrating your departure.

You look around the house and see potential everywhere.

The bedroom that held trophies, posters, and questionable laundry habits becomes... something else.

A home office.
A yoga room.
A craft space.
A reading nook.
A gym you will use eventually.

You are very optimistic during this phase.

The bunk beds come out. The desk stays. The door gets repainted. You tell people you're repurposing the space, which sounds intentional and not at all emotional. You mean it, too. Mostly.

And then — occasionally — you find yourself standing in the doorway longer than necessary.

Not sad.
Just… paused.

Boomers are very good at pretending we are fine. We've had practice. We grew up learning how to keep moving. How to adapt. How not to linger too long on anything that might slow us down.

But empty nesting has a way of reopening old emotional files you didn't realize were still accessible.

You remember the good days vividly. The routines. The noise. The chaos that felt endless at the time and now feels oddly comforting in hindsight. The messes you complained about. The interruptions you negotiated around. The presence you took for granted because it felt permanent.

You don't want it back.

You just want to remember it accurately.

This is also when romance gets a second look.

Not a reboot.
A recalibration.

Suddenly, it's just the two of you again. Or just you. No audience. No interruptions. No homework questions mid-sentence. You remember what it's like to finish a thought without circling back to it later.

For couples, this can feel surprisingly intimate — and surprisingly unfamiliar.

Some rediscover each other with enthusiasm. There's curiosity again. Playfulness. Time. You can leave the house without planning three days in advance. You can talk without whispering. You can sit quietly together without feeling like something needs to be managed.

Others approach this phase with caution. You've both changed. Of course you have. Years happened. Responsibilities happened. Versions of yourselves emerged that never needed to be compared because there wasn't time.

That's okay.

You don't have to pretend it's 1978.
You don't have to pick up where you left off.
You get to meet where you are now.

Date nights return.
So do early bedtimes.

Both can be romantic.

For single Boomers, the reset feels different — but no less significant. The house is quiet, but it's yours. Valentine's Day no longer requires explanation or compromise. You can celebrate it. Ignore it. Redefine it. Or use it as a perfectly reasonable excuse to buy excellent chocolate and enjoy it without commentary.

Many Boomers do exactly that.

Some rediscover hobbies they forgot they liked. Others rediscover the joy of doing absolutely nothing on purpose. The extra room becomes a place for creativity, reflection, or simply storage for things you're not ready to decide about yet.

That counts too.

This phase of life invites honesty — the quiet kind.

You can miss your children and still enjoy the quiet.
You can love the memories and still want the space.
You can wish for the old days and still be deeply grateful they're over.

None of this is contradictory.
It's layered.

Empty nesting isn't an ending. It's a reset. A chance to edit your life without starting from scratch. To choose what stays. What goes. What gets another try. What you no longer need to carry just because you always have.

Valentine's Day during this phase feels lighter. Less loaded. More optional. It's no longer a test or a performance. It's just a day — one you can fill with whatever feels right now, not what once did.

Dinner out.
Dinner in.
Friends.
Silence.
Laughter that doesn't have to be quiet.

Boomers enter this chapter with perspective. We've loved deeply. We've worried endlessly. We've raised people who now belong to the world, not just to us.

That matters.

And now, in ways both subtle and significant, we get to belong to ourselves again.

Not completely.

But enough.

Enough to breathe.
Enough to choose.
Enough to enjoy what comes next without apologizing for wanting it.

Headphones still on.

This is where it gets interesting.

♥ CHAPTER VIII

Still Interested: Valentine's Day, With Fewer Rules
and Better Snacks

This is the chapter where Valentine's Day loosens
its grip.

Not because we stopped caring.
Because we finally stopped auditioning.

There was a time when Valentine's Day felt like a
performance review. A quiet but relentless one.
You were assessed on effort, presentation,
originality, and follow-through. Someone,
somewhere, was always judging — even if that
someone was just you, standing in a drugstore aisle

holding two cards and wondering which one made you look sane.

Too much sentiment felt risky.
Too little felt careless.
Funny could backfire.
Serious could feel like a commitment you hadn't fully thought through.

You learned to read cards the way you read people — looking for subtext, tone, unintended consequences. You knew which ones tried too hard. You knew which ones played it safe. You knew which ones said nothing but cost more, which felt like a commentary all its own.

That phase has passed.

Not dramatically. Not ceremoniously. It just… loosened. Somewhere along the way, the pressure softened. The stakes lowered. The need to get it "right" gave way to the freedom to get it honest.

Boomers arrive here with experience. With perspective. With a finely tuned sense of what matters and an even sharper sense of what absolutely does not. Valentine's Day, once a high-stakes event with emotional penalties, now feels more like an invitation.

And invitations, at this age, are optional.

You can accept it.
You can decline it.
You can reschedule it.
You can quietly modify it until it fits the life you're actually living — not the one you were once supposed to want.

That's not indifference.

That's freedom.

Still interested does not mean desperate.
It means awake.

It means you're present enough to notice desire when it shows up — and secure enough not to panic about it. You no longer mistake intensity for importance. You

no longer assume urgency equals depth. You've lived long enough to know that the loudest thing in the room is rarely the most meaningful.

Attraction doesn't need to knock loudly to be real. Sometimes it just sits down.

Romance at this stage is less about fireworks and more about warmth. Less spectacle. More substance. Less proving. More enjoying. You're not building a story anymore. You're living one.

Sometimes that something is another person —
familiar or new, known or surprising.

Sometimes it's the luxury of peace — real peace,
not the kind you used to promise yourself once
everything else was handled.

Peace that arrives without conditions.

Peace that doesn't require a plan.

Valentine's Day during this phase can actually be
fun again. And that might be the most unexpected
part. There's laughter now — not the tight,
performative laughter of earlier years, but the easy
kind. The kind that comes out when no one is
trying too hard or trying to impress.

Plans get made without pressure. Or not made at
all.

Affection arrives without a script. Or an agenda.

You can flirt without needing an outcome.

You can enjoy attention without overanalyzing it later.

You can say no without rehearsing an explanation in your head.

That's not cynicism.

That's fluency.

It's knowing the language well enough to stop translating every sentence. It's recognizing when something feels good and letting that be enough. It's trusting your own responses instead of checking them against some invisible standard.

But this chapter isn't all ease and lightness. It can't be. Because nothing we carry at this age is uncomplicated.

This is also the chapter where we acknowledge what didn't make it here.

Boomers carry history. Not just personal history — national history. Collective history. Loss that doesn't evaporate just because the calendar flips. Wars were fought. Towers fell. Lives changed in moments that still echo, whether we talk about them or not.

Some Valentine's Days arrived in the shadow of events that rearranged everything — publicly and privately. Some years, celebration felt almost inappropriate. Other years, it felt necessary in a way that was hard to explain.

Some Boomers lost partners to time.
Some to illness.

Some to circumstance.
Some to history itself.

Valentine's Day can feel complicated when love has been interrupted by forces larger than any one relationship. When memory shares space with longing. When celebration feels layered — not heavy, just dimensional.

There is no wrong way to hold that.

Grief doesn't cancel joy.
Memory doesn't disqualify pleasure.
Absence doesn't erase love.

This is where the single Boomer enters the conversation — not as an afterthought, not as a consolation prize, but as a fully realized participant in life. Single by choice. Single by loss. Single by timing. Single by survival.

Single by having lived long enough to know that status is not the same thing as substance.

Valentine's Day does not belong exclusively to couples. It never did. It was marketed that way, but marketing is not authority. Boomers, of all people, know the difference between a campaign and the truth.

Single Boomers understand this instinctively.You celebrate yourself now. Or your friends. Or the people who showed up when it mattered — the ones who stayed, the ones who checked in, the ones who know your history without needing footnotes.

You make reservations for joy instead of obligation.
You buy flowers because you like them.
You eat chocolate because you earned it — not because it symbolizes anything, but because it's good.

Sometimes Valentine's Day is dinner with someone you love romantically.

Sometimes it's lunch with a girlfriend who knows your entire story and doesn't need context.

Sometimes it's quiet — deliberately quiet, the kind that feels chosen.

And sometimes it's all of that at once.

Still interested also means still capable of hope — but not dependent on it. You don't need the day to deliver something in order for it to be worthwhile. You can enjoy what's in front of you without insisting it turn into something else.

That's maturity.
Not resignation.

Boomers don't romanticize the past anymore. We remember it clearly. The good. The hard. The parts that didn't work. The moments that felt important at the time and the ones that turned out to be. That honesty lightens the present. It removes the

pressure to recreate something that only existed once because you were younger, less informed, and still guessing.

Valentine's Day at this stage feels less like a demand and more like a suggestion.

You take what you want.
You leave the rest.
You know the difference.

And if there's laughter now — real laughter, the kind that surprises you — it's because you've lived long enough to recognize joy when it shows up quietly and asks to stay. You don't interrogate it anymore.
You don't test it.
You don't ask where it's going.

You just let it sit with you for a while.

🖤 CHAPTER IX

In Defense of Chocolate: A Brief, Necessary Intermission

Before we get serious — and we will — we need to talk about chocolate.

Not philosophically.
Not academically.
Personally.

Because Valentine's Day without chocolate is just February with better marketing.

Chocolate has been carrying an unreasonable amount of emotional labor for decades. It has been asked to apologize for romance that didn't quite show up. To stand in for effort when words failed. To soften disappointment. To act as a peace offering. To occasionally rescue a relationship that needed more than cocoa and a ribbon.

That is a lot to put on a bean.

And yet.

Chocolate holds up.

It always has.

Chocolate is not just candy. That's the mistake people make when they dismiss it. Chocolate is chemistry. Chocolate is comfort. Chocolate is ritual. Chocolate is one of the few indulgences that arrives with legitimate benefits and absolutely no requirement to explain yourself.

Chocolate improves mood. It doesn't ask why you need it. Chocolate lowers stress. It doesn't ask follow-up questions. Chocolate encourages happiness. It doesn't demand proof.

This alone makes it superior to most things we've dated.

Chocolate doesn't interrogate your choices. It doesn't suggest improvements. It doesn't imply you could have done better if you'd just tried harder. It meets you exactly where you are — tired, content, reflective, celebratory, or quietly done for the day.

Which makes it the perfect Valentine.

Dark chocolate, especially, has earned a respectable reputation over the years. It's been studied. Analyzed. Spoken of kindly by people in lab coats who tend not to say nice things unless they have data. It's associated with heart health, antioxidants, improved blood flow, and that subtle but unmistakable sense that things might be okay after all.

Milk chocolate has fewer credentials but far more enthusiasm. It shows up eager. Reliable. Comforting. It knows what it is and doesn't pretend otherwise.

White chocolate is here for emotional support. It doesn't claim to be serious. It just wants to be invited.

All of them count.

Valentine's Day gives you permission — official, stamped, notarized, and quietly reinforced by every store display — to indulge for one day without commentary. One day. That's it. Not a lifestyle. Not a statement. A moment.

And considering that spring doesn't officially show up for another five weeks, chocolate is essentially seasonal emotional insulation. We are not overdoing it.
We are preparing.

Chocolate has sound, and this matters more than people admit.

The snap of a good chocolate bar is confidence. It says this was made properly.
The crinkle of the wrapper is anticipation. It's the sound of permission being granted.
The soft thud of a box placed on the counter is intention. It means someone thought ahead — even if that someone was you.

Chocolate announces itself gently. It doesn't shout. It doesn't rush. It doesn't demand an audience. It melts on its own timeline, which Boomers respect deeply.

We have learned to respect anything that refuses to be hurried.

Chocolate is also remarkably inclusive.

Sweetheart.
No sweetheart.
New sweetheart.
Old sweetheart.
Complicated sweetheart.

Sweetheart who lives in another time zone and texts inconsistently.

Chocolate does not discriminate.

You don't need a date to enjoy it. You don't need a plan. You don't even technically need Valentine's Day — though it helps with the justification and the packaging. Chocolate works just as well alone, with friends, after dinner, before dinner, or standing at the kitchen counter wondering how your life ended up here and deciding, with some relief, that it's actually fine.

Boomers understand this instinctively.

We have eaten chocolate in celebration.
We have eaten it in consolation.
We have eaten it quietly, without ceremony, because the day asked too much.

Chocolate pairs beautifully with laughter.

Laughter that says, We survived.
Laughter that says, This is good enough.
Laughter that says, I am not explaining this to anyone.

Boomers understand indulgence differently now. We are not reckless. We are intentional. We know the difference between enjoyment and excess. We know when something is a moment and not a habit. We know when pleasure is a pause, not an escape.

Valentine's Day is a pause.

Chocolate belongs here.

It doesn't need to be shared to be meaningful.
It doesn't need to be hidden to be enjoyed.
It doesn't need a narrative.

Eat it slowly. Or don't.
Share it if you want. Or don't.
Save the good piece for last. Or eat it first, because you've earned that choice.

Let it melt.
Let it pass.

Let yourself enjoy something uncomplicated before we move on to caring for the one heart that has been with you through every chapter of this story — through the noise, the changes, the surprises, the recalibrations.

Because joy counts.

Laughter counts.

And sometimes the healthiest thing you can do is unwrap something shiny, take a bite, and not overthink it.

We'll get serious next.

But not yet.

Headphones still on.

Chocolate within reach.

♥ CHAPTER X

Handle With Care: A Valentine for the Rest of the Year

Here's where we slow down.

Not because the fun is over — it isn't — but because this is the part that actually lasts. The part that doesn't wilt, melt, or get marked down on February fifteenth. This is the Valentine that doesn't come in a box. The one you carry forward whether you mean to or not.

Boomers have lived through a lot.

That's not a dramatic statement. It's just accurate.

We've lived through wars that shaped our childhoods and conflicts that reshaped our adulthood. We've lived through recessions, recoveries, and the uneasy space in between. We've watched cultural revolutions rise, settle, and rise again under different names. We've survived technological whiplash — from rotary phones to pocket-sized computers that can tell us how many steps we didn't take today.

We adapted.

Then adapted again.

Then adapted to the adaptation.

And through all of it, our hearts just kept going.

Sometimes under stress.

Sometimes under joy.

Sometimes under pressure we didn't name out loud because there were other things to handle first.

Heart health isn't an abstract concept to Boomers. It's not a brochure. It's not a headline. It's personal. It shows up in exam rooms. In family histories that suddenly feel closer than they used to. In conversations that lower their voices without anyone asking them to.

We know the language now. We didn't always, but we do now. Blood pressure. Cholesterol. Activity levels. Risk factors. Numbers that get written down and circled. We've heard them. We've lived alongside them. We've learned that the heart is both remarkably strong and surprisingly sensitive.

That combination feels familiar.

The good news — and there is good news — is that caring for your heart isn't about becoming someone else. It doesn't require perfection. It doesn't demand reinvention. It asks for attention.

Not obsession.
Not fear.
Attention.

Boomers understand attention. We've been paying attention our whole lives. To children. To work. To responsibilities that didn't come with instructions. We know how to show up. We just haven't always aimed that skill inward.

Our bodies tell the truth now. They speak more clearly. Sometimes more loudly than we'd prefer. Bones creak a little more than they used to. Joints offer commentary. Energy has opinions. But here's the thing we don't say often enough:

They still move.

Movement looks different now. It's not about conquering anything. It's not about training for an event. It's about staying in the game. Walking because it clears your head. Stretching because it feels good afterward. Dancing in the kitchen because a song came on and you remembered how to move that way.

Parking a little farther away.
Taking the long route on purpose.
Choosing motion because stillness has had enough airtime.

This isn't about discipline.
It's about participation.

Chocolate, as we've already agreed, remains part of the conversation. Moderation isn't deprivation. It's discernment. A little dark chocolate fits just fine into a life that includes pleasure and intention. Especially when it's paired with laughter — real laughter — the kind that settles your breathing without effort.

Stress reduction isn't a footnote. It's a strategy. Boomers know stress. We've carried it quietly. We've managed it efficiently. We've normalized it when it should have raised questions. Learning to soften it now isn't indulgence. It's maintenance.

And February matters.

Valentine's Day opens the door.
Heart Month holds it open.

There's something quietly brilliant about that timing. Romance followed immediately by reality. Celebration followed by care. One day focused outward, the next month gently turning the attention back in.

So here's a thought — not a directive, not a rule, just a distinctly Boomer-sized idea.

Let February fifteenth be Heart New Year.

The day after the candy.
The day after the pressure.
The day after the performance.

A reset that doesn't involve guilt or declarations or promises you don't intend to keep. Just a pause. A moment to notice where you are and what you want to carry forward.

Boomers don't need grand overhauls. We've lived long enough to know they rarely last. What sticks is what fits. What integrates. What feels reasonable on a Tuesday.

Sustainability matters to us because we've seen what happens when it's ignored. We've watched trends flare and vanish. Miracle fixes rise and fail. What remains is what you can live with — not heroically, just honestly.

And real life, for Boomers, includes connection.

We are the generation that remembers dialing a phone and now sends messages without thinking about the mechanics at all. We've seen electric cars, driverless cars, and ideas that once lived in science fiction become part of traffic. We adjusted. Again.

Which means we know how to reach people.

Sometimes it's a text that doesn't need context.
Sometimes it's a call you've been meaning to make.
Sometimes it's an email that just says, Thinking of you.

Connection isn't sentimental. It's structural.

Loneliness isn't a personal failure. It's a health factor. We know this now in ways we didn't when we were younger and busier and surrounded by noise. Community matters. Familiar voices matter. Shared laughter matters — especially the kind that doesn't require explanation.

Boomers have always known how to reach out.

We just do it more deliberately now.

Valentine's Day doesn't end on February fourteenth. It hands the conversation forward. To February fifteenth. To Heart New Year. To a steadier, quieter form of care that doesn't need witnesses.

Whatever you choose to do for your New Heart Health, New Boomer Year — do it kindly. Do it realistically. Do it with the understanding that you've already lived through more change than anyone could have predicted.

Your heart has been with you through all of it.

Through the stress.
Through the joy.
Through the years you didn't think about it at all.

It deserves your attention now.

Not fearfully.
Not obsessively.
Wisely.

That's not a slogan.

That's lived experience.

That's the Boomer way.

Headphones still on.

The room still quiet.

This one's for the rest of the year.

🖤 ONE LAST THING

If this were actually a podcast, this is the moment when the music would start to come back in.

Not loudly.
Just enough to let you know we're landing.

I'd probably clear my throat. Maybe laugh quietly at something I forgot to say. I might thank a sponsor that doesn't exist. And then I'd do the thing all podcasters do when they realize they've been talking for a long time to someone they can't see.

I'd say thank you.

Because if you're here — if you've read this far — you weren't skimming. You were listening. In your own way. With your own pauses. Your own memories chiming in when something landed a little too close to home.

This was a podcast you didn't have to charge.
You could stop and start whenever you wanted.

You could reread something without pretending you caught it the first time.

No earbuds required.
No algorithm involved.
Just you, a book, and a familiar rhythm.

That felt right for this conversation.

Boomers understand this format instinctively. We grew up with radio voices in kitchens, cars, and bedrooms. We know what it means to listen without watching. To stay with a voice because it feels companionable. Because it's saying something you recognize, even if you hadn't put it into words yet.

This book wasn't meant to tell you anything you don't already know.

It was meant to sit beside you and say, Yes. That. Exactly.

If something made you laugh, good.
If something made you pause, even better.
If something made you feel less alone in a thought you assumed was only yours — then this worked.

So thank you for tuning in.

Thank you for staying.

Thank you for listening all the way to the end.

You can close the book now.

Or just sit with it for a minute.

Either way — same channel, same frequency.

Until next time.

ACKNOWLEDGMENTS

This book exists because of love in its many forms — the kind that stays, the kind that leaves, and the kind that never really goes anywhere.

To my high school sweetheart, who later became my spouse for thirty-eight years:
my soul still knows your shape.
I miss you in the quiet moments, in the loud laughter, and in all the ordinary days we thought would last forever.

To my dear junior high and high school friend, Brenda — you were there when everything felt first and important. You are missed more than you know, and remembered more than you'd probably be comfortable with.

To my school friends Nelda, Frances, Renée, and Judy — thank you for the years when everything was forming. Those early friendships taught me how to listen, how to laugh, and how to be myself long before I knew who that was. I didn't always get it right, but you were part of the learning.

To my later friends — Barbeta, Jennifer, Lisa, Sharon, Hazel, and Ashley.   My tennis duo Salt & Pepper — even when we don't see or talk as often as we could, the connection remains. Time and distance have refined what matters, and I carry you with me in ways that don't require constant contact.

To my lifelong friend, Wendy, of sixty-eight years — you are living proof that time does not weaken connection; it deepens it. You have been the constant thread through every version of me, and for that I am endlessly grateful.

With love, gratitude, and just enough wit to keep things honest,

🖤

REFERENCES

Hallmark Cards, Inc. History of Hallmark Cards.
https://corporate.hallmark.com/about/hallmark-cards-
company/history/

Hallmark Cards, Inc. Founding and Early Years (1910s–
1950s).
https://corporate.hallmark.com/about/hallmark-cards-
company/history/founding-1910s/

Hallmark. History of Valentine's Day.
https://ideas.hallmark.com/articles/valentines-day-ideas/
history-of-valentines-day/

The Barnes Foundation. The Origins of the Commercial
Valentine.
https://www.thebarnesmuseum.org/blog/before-hallmark-
the-origins-of-the-commercialization-of-valentines-day-
cards-in-the-victorian-era

Governing. The Once and Future Shopping Mall.
https://www.governing.com/urban/the-once-and-future-
shopping-mall

Business Insider. History of Southdale Center, the First Modern American Mall.
https://www.businessinsider.com/first-shopping-mall-us-southdale-center-history-photos-2017-8

International Council of Shopping Centers. Why the Core Appeal of Malls Endures.
https://www.icsc.com/news-and-views/icsc-exchange/from-southdale-center-to-gen-z-why-the-core-appeal-of-malls-endures

AAA Foundation for Traffic Safety. Nationwide Review of Graduated Driver Licensing.
https://aaafoundation.org/wp-content/uploads/2018/02/NationwideReviewOfGDLReport.pdf

National Highway Traffic Safety Administration. Graduated Driver Licensing Systems.
https://www.nhtsa.gov/document/traffic-safety-facts-laws-graduated-driver-licensing-system

Insurance Institute for Highway Safety. Teen Drivers: Research Overview.
https://www.iihs.org/research-areas/teenagers

Insurance Information Institute. Background on Teen Drivers.
https://www.iii.org/article/background-on-teen-drivers

Centers for Disease Control and Prevention. Graduated Driver Licensing and Nighttime Restrictions.
https://www.cdc.gov/mmwr/volumes/65/wr/mm6529a1.htm

The Wall Street Journal. Empty Nesters Reclaim the Kids' Rooms.
https://eberlein.com/wp-content/uploads/2021/11/Empty-Nesters-Reclaim-the-Kids-Rooms-WSJ.html

AARP. Lifestyle and Financial Patterns of Empty Nesters.
https://www.aarp.org/money/personal-finance/empty-nester-financial-mistakes/

Cleveland Clinic. Health Benefits of Dark Chocolate.
https://health.clevelandclinic.org/dark-chocolate-health-benefits

Harvard T.H. Chan School of Public Health. Dark Chocolate and Cardiovascular Health.
https://www.hsph.harvard.edu/news/dark-chocolate-health-flavonoids/

Harvard Health Publishing. Chocolate, Arteries, and Blood Pressure.
https://www.health.harvard.edu/staying-healthy/dark-chocolate-protects-arteries

Ried, K., et al. "Effect of Cocoa on Blood Pressure: Meta-Analysis." BMC Medicine.
https://pubmed.ncbi.nlm.nih.gov/20584271/

Desch, S., et al. "Cocoa Products and Cardiovascular Risk Factors."
https://pubmed.ncbi.nlm.nih.gov/19910929/

American Heart Association. Heart Disease and Stroke Statistics Update.
https://www.heart.org/en/about-us/heart-and-stroke-association-statistics

American Heart Association. Older Adults and Cardiovascular Disease.
https://professional.heart.org/en/science-news/heart-disease-and-stroke-statistics

American Heart Association. American Heart Month.
https://www.heart.org/en/american-heart-month

Centers for Disease Control and Prevention. Heart Disease Facts and Statistics.
https://www.cdc.gov/heart-disease/data-research/facts-stats

National Heart, Lung, and Blood Institute. American Heart Month.
https://www.nhlbi.nih.gov/education/american-heart-month

www.ingramcontent.com/pod-product-compliance
Lightning Source LLC
Chambersburg PA
CBHW022123280326
41933CB00007B/514